Course for Total Health

SELF-RELIANCE AND CONSTRUCTIVE CHANGE

The Declaration of Spiritual Independence

by Hua-Ching Ni

SEVEN STAR
COMMUNICATIONS
Santa Monica, CA

SevenStar Communications Group, Inc.
1314 Second Street
Santa Monica, California 90401

Acknowledgements: Thanks to Suta Cahill for editing, Janet DeCourtney for desktop publishing, Arthur Sutherland for designing the cover and to many friends for proofreading.

First Printing May 1995

It is recommended that you study Hua-Ching Ni's other books and materials for further knowledge about a healthy lifestyle and to learn other practices. There are no claims for absolute effectiveness of the material in this booklet, which is to be used at your own discretion.

The College of Tao offers teachings about health, spirituality and the Integral Way based on the teachings of Hua-Ching Ni. To obtain information about the Integral Way of Life Correspondence Course, please write the College of Tao, PO Box 1222, El Prado, NM 87529 USA or call (310) 576-1902. To obtain information about Mentors teaching in your area or country, please write the Universal Society of the Integral Way, PO Box 28993, Atlanta, GA 30358-0993.

Library of Congress Cataloging-in-Publication Data

Ni, Hua Ching.
    Self-reliance and constructive change : the declaration of
spiritual independence / by Hua-Ching Ni.
         p. c. -- (Course for total health)
      ISBN 0-937064-85-8 (pbk. : alk. paper)
      1. Spiritual life. 2. Spiritual life-- Taoism. I. Title. II.
Series.
      BL624.N4888   1995   95-10463
      299'.51444--dc20   CIP

T
A O

**Truth Above Oneself
Truth Among Ourselves**

Contents

*This booklet is dedicated to
those who value spiritual self-reliance
and assist the positive change of the world.*

INTRODUCTION TO
THE COURSE FOR TOTAL HEALTH

I

Life is the convergence of natural energy.
Through evolution, it finds progress.

The spiritual path is not an external path. It is the path of continually developing life. The subjective effort for a better life is instinctive to most people, causing their latent self-consciousness to be expressed in external pursuits. The ancient culture of China expressed this human effort in a natural way that is unique among all other cultures and religions in that its central focus was immortal life. Ancient sages discovered that spiritual energy, which is internal energy, is the source of health and of a long and happy life, when suitably strengthened and expressed.

The purpose of this series is to introduce this great body of knowledge to you. Since it is not organized as a religion, its pragmatic value in your life is your health. People live to increase their health, and in turn their health serves their happiness. This is the most conspicuous illustration of the law of causality. The effect of doing right is to reward our life and by doing wrong we punish ourselves. This is a direct correlation that all people must face, no one can evade it.

These teachings can serve you throughout your life. They are the fruit of millions of years of attainment by people whose long lives received the natural support of their immortal souls.

II

The basic motive of life is to find happiness, and health is an important part of that happiness. How, then, do you improve your health? Take more pills, go to more doctors, spend more time at the spa? Ancient people did not have such resources, yet records clearly show that there were individuals who lived to be over a hundred years old and who experienced a state of health so complete that their strength and ability were considered supernatural.

1

In the *Course for Total Health* series, I will show you how health is related to more than just your physical body. Your health is affected, more than you may realize, by your mental and cultural attitudes, by your religious upbringing, and by environmental influences, including that of the society in which you live.

"No," many of you may be thinking, "my problem is that I need more vitamins or antibiotics." I do not wish to stop you from consulting your physician, but please read these booklets to get at the root of what can help bring you total happiness, health, well-being and success. Vitamins alone cannot bring happiness or health. Health comes from strong internal energy, which can also be called spiritual energy. People in ancient China worked to strengthen their spiritual energy in order to improve their lives and their health in totally natural ways. My work in the *Course for Total Health* is to introduce their great knowledge to you.

III

The first volume in this series, *Self-Reliance and Constructive Change*, discusses how being attached to cultural and religious fashions can hinder personal health and how you can go about detaching yourself from their influence.

The second volume, *The Power of Positive Living*, offers new ideas about simple improvements that can be made in everyday life to increase your positive energy and thus your health.

The third volume, *The Universal Path of Natural Life*, gives you simple guidelines for a natural, healthy personality, which is so rarely seen in these confused modern times.

The fourth volume, *The Natural Course of Spiritual Life: the Law of Causality*, is about changing your behavior and thoughts in order to create positive effects in your life to a degree you would never have thought possible. This includes health, wealth, happiness, better relationships, etc.

The fifth volume, *The Inner Source of Creative Life*, is a dialogue between myself and students who understand that health is not only skin deep and who ask questions about how to best focus their energies to improve their lives.

The sixth volume, *The Universal Mind*, discusses the connection between your conscious mind and the creative, empowering force that runs the Universe: the universal mind. Increasing and enhancing this connection will awaken the power of healthy creativity within you.

The seventh volume, *The Universal Divine One*, contains the key to spiritual health and explains how uniting your life spirit with the divine spirit will elevate your life to a higher potential.

There will be more to come!

INTRODUCTION TO
SELF-RELIANCE AND
CONSTRUCTIVE CHANGE

There are three types of civilizations in the world. The type with which people are most familiar is religious civilization. In western history, this is represented by the culture of the Middle Ages. The second type is intellectual civilization. This type has become accepted in the everyday lives of most people through academic achievement and modern technology and includes modern democracy.

There is a third type of civilization that has been forgotten or has become less obvious, but no one can live without it. It has been expressed in slightly different ways at different times, and it is the foundation of life. It is the ancient natural civilization. It could also be called "humanistic civilization." This kind of civilization was developed and maintained in China until 1949, when the natural lifestyle of a million year old society was brutally and ruthlessly destroyed.

Humanistic civilization is what I teach. It differs greatly from modern civilization, which tends toward an impersonal, over-materialized view of life. Ancient people used the word *Tao* to express it. *Tao* means nature itself, or the Way of nature. We live it every day of our lives, it is not a concept.

The function of a natural humanistic civilization is to awaken those who have been misled by social or religious fantasies and to help them improve their lives. By counteracting the trend of intellectual overexpansion, which tends to neglect the natural spiritual reality of life, natural humanistic civilization offers people a central path of life: it recognizes the physical foundation of the body, the subtle level of mind, and the even more subtle sphere of spirit or soul.

Religious civilization is for immature people who are at a stage in which they cannot take spiritual responsibility for their own lives. They need an external means of support to maintain their moral standards and provide a positive focus for their lives. Very simply, they need social discipline.

According to the standard of natural life, religion goes against human nature. It is like adding a sixth finger to your hand. Such appendages are shackles on human nature. They are not natural, they are not indicative of spiritual development, they are not equivalent to spiritual self-awareness and they do not induce spiritual responsibility in life. Their value is shallow and temporal.

As all of you know, I respect the universal truth of nature, which is not partial. When I came to the West, however, the general public categorized my teachings as a religion, yet those who have studied them deeply have come to understand that my teaching helps restore the naturalness of human life and one's spiritual nature. It does not add something to your life, but removes the accumulated toxins of cultural misconceptions so that you can appreciate the natural civilization that is ageless. In other words, I promote a healthy spiritual life, a healthy natural life and a healthy life of the mind that creates no real conflict with any culture or religion. Such a life is deeper, more practical, and more beneficial than any man made phenomenon.

Tao is nature itself, which cannot truly be interpreted; thus, I call my teaching the Universal Way of Natural Spiritual Development for All People. It can be shortened to the Integral Way, the Universal Way or the Gentle Way. The most accurate description, however, is still *Tao* or nature itself.

When people call my teachings Taoism or call me a Taoist Master, I am not particularly bothered, because it represents their level of social understanding. However, it is my duty to clarify their understanding. The purpose of my teaching is to remove whatever obstacle you have to seeing the naturalness of life.

For many decades, I have worked on one subject: teaching the natural subtle truth of the Universe and all people. I present my work for your evaluation. May it enable you to make a big step forward, spiritually and mentally, toward union with nature itself, with *Tao*, the Way, the Subtle Law of the Universe and the subtle substance of universal life.

The natural foundation of life should be respected and valued for the further evolution of life. Nobody should neglect the subtle projection that brings forth the future of humankind as an impartial projection of universal nature.

Nature inspires people in different generations and different places. The American forefathers were naturally inspired to live their own lives and construct their own society. You might think they were inspired by their religions, but I believe they were inspired by nature itself to become the founders of a natural civilization. They were Taoist in their bones; they were much more than religious followers.

The main article in this booklet is the "Declaration of Spiritual Independence," which was spiritually inspired by Thomas Jefferson. The next step beyond political independence is the spiritual independence of all people. One day, all national, cultural and religious boundaries will break down, and there will be a universal citizenship with universal love, and all people will enjoy liberty and the all-fulfilling naturalness of life.

SPIRITUAL INDEPENDENCE
AND THE NATURAL TRUTH OF LIFE

Charlottesville, Virginia
Sunday, October 23, 1994

The American forerunners who came to this land were seeking accurate spiritual expression rather than another conventional social religion. Around 200 years ago, in writing the Declaration of Independence for a new United States of America, Thomas Jefferson brought hope for a new society. His Declaration captured some of the spiritual direction of our forefathers, but it concentrated for the most part on the political aspect of society rather than a totally spiritually focused view of life. Thus we continue his effort by offering the following Declaration of Spiritual Independence at a time when people's intellectual development is sufficient to meet their spiritual stature. They also have developed themselves and met one another in this place where Thomas Jefferson was born and lived.

The Declaration
of Spiritual Independence

It is self-evident that the Universe developed by its own nature. No human mind intervened. No religion can proclaim that before the Universe existed there was a man-like will at work. The Universe developed by itself. Human spirits, or mind, came much later and the human capability of mental recognition came even later. The human mind has no experience of the prenatal stage of the Universe. No mythology of creation is valid or can be trusted as a belief.

The Universe is spiritual in nature, thus humans too are spiritual by nature. This is the inner truth. However, a spiritual nature is something to be developed rather than a simple gift to be

7

received. Human spiritual functions include intuition, inspiration, reflection and imaging through visions or dreams. By no means do these constitute the foundation of a rigid religion. The religious tendencies of the human mind at a certain stage became socially oriented rather than natural and spiritual. The dualistic approach to God as separate from people has become an obstacle for the growth of the human spirit. The darkness of religion has suffocated the natural spiritual growth of the human race for 3,000 years. Freedom, independence and naturalness are what support the true growth of all people.

The universal subtle truth is valid for all people, whether they are religious believers or not. The universal subtle law is naturally responsive, without the need of intervention by any level of being. Universal subtle energy is the substance of the Universe and all lives; it is omnipresent, omnipotent and all-knowing. These truths have been usurped by religions to establish the authority of their churches and their priests, but by no means can natural reality be monopolized by a group of people who lack pure motives.

Human wisdom is what enables people to live in harmony with the universal subtle law. One can take a fairly peaceful ride on the universal subtle energy in a flowing manner to accomplish one's natural life and further development.

The Universe is integral. The spiritual energy of the Universe is integral. The wisdom of such truth is integral. Thus, the Way is integral and the Universal Integral Way serves the growth of all people. The spiritual value and correct fulfillment of the Integral Way can only be realized in secular life. No other way is truthfully the spiritual way.

No religion has the power or authority to judge or control people's souls. Each individual's spiritual effort should be independent and not coerced. Any life that offers humanistic benefit and universal love to the world is an expression of the universal divine nature. The contributions of religious teachers, on the other hand, are hollow by comparison.

The deep and correct spiritual expression which was taught by the American founding fathers is freedom or independence from conventional religions and spiritual self-reliance on natural learning and self-development. Universal life is on the path of self-completion and accomplishment. Thus, I, a humble universal spiritual worker, proclaim the Declaration of the Natural Spiritual Truth of Life of awakened souls on Earth to be the following:

The Natural Spiritual Truth of Life

1. The three natural gifts of all individuals include:

complete body
capable intellect
precious soul

The only creator is nature. Nature is divine. All divinity is the subtle fact of nature.

2. All lives are supported by the Earth. Earth is supported by the vast sky which forms the Universe. The inner nature of the Universe, from the subtlest to the most solid of phenomena, is a thoroughfare. This thoroughfare is called Universal Nature, the Universal Subtle Law, or the Integral Way.

3. The Universe is a big piece of energy. Human life is a small piece of energy. The big and the small share the same essence and nature. They both abide within the subtle law.

4. Through internal observation we can realize that the big life and the small life are one life. Through external observation what

we learn is that all individuality is interrelated. At the deepest level, we learn that a state of absolute separation is not possible, although individual independence is possible and this can even further one's development.

5. To align oneself with the universal nature is the way to live and continue to develop. To deviate from universal nature is to go astray and become extinct.

6. The most important provision that nature has bestowed upon all lives is free will. Freedom is meant for development, not for negative indulgence. This freedom for development comes from the natural foundation of each life. There is no limitation to anyone's potential development.

7. The Universe evolved from chaos to order. Human leaders, however, repeatedly attempt to turn order into chaos. Chaos is brought about by the competition between leaders, and the participation of their followers in this competition. Sometimes progress is seen, but for the most part it is a waste.

Natural progress is the subtle evolution of the old order to become a new order. To reduce the amount of sacrifice involved in the process of change, keep away from chaos but keep good orderliness. This is how an individual can develop oneself. To follow the natural progression of subtle change is a mark of high civilization. To engage in competition and its resulting chaos is barbarism.

8. If there is a natural disaster, it is not the result of a divine plan or response to human behavior. It is simply a natural disaster.

It is the responsibility of humankind to develop the spiritual sense and intellectual capacity to foresee and then evade or face a natural disaster; taking inspiration from natural divinity and the spiritual sphere of life which are not disturbed by such things. Natural phenomena were incorrectly construed by old religions to promote fear and obedience, without revealing the correct foundation of the facts.

9. Nurturing one's individual spiritual sensibility and nurturing a spiritual sensibility of one's natural surroundings enables a person to know and then react correctly to all life situations. Peace is the highest nutrition for one's sensibilities.

10. The alternation of yin and yang shapes the pattern of nature. This is valid in all spheres of nature, yet yin and yang should not be rigidly interpreted by the human mind, because yin can be yang and yang can also be yin in order to fulfill the creative cooperation of nature.

11. We believe that a good life is possible for all people, because a good life can be attained by individual and social effort. An individual's worldly attainment is connected with both their personal potential and their social environment. When these meet, success and prosperity are possible. Without them, personal struggle alone is fruitless. Without them, it is better to improve oneself and allow progress to happen of its own accord.

The foundation of a good life is the joint growth of the individual and society. Each individual should develop his or her natural potential for healthy life expression and not evade the natural responsibilities of life such as work and marriage. Marriage is for the purpose of raising children, and teamwork is for productivity and the health of life. One should do away with any unnatural influences coming from oneself or from society.

12. Have no fear of life and death. No one has ever been able to refuse natural transformation, yet it is one's personal responsibility

to do away with unnatural influences that harm one's natural health and joy of life.

It is the way of general people to use the subtle sphere of life to pursue the attainment of fame and wealth in the apparent sphere of life. This is spiritual undevelopment. The natural fulfillment of a developed life is to nurture the development of the subtle sphere of life. This is spiritually healthy and is the approach of developed people.

The apparent sphere of life is short-lived, but the subtle sphere is long-lived. An incorrect exchange of subtle force for apparent attainment is inappropriate. Those who practice the principle of balance in the fulfillment of all aspects of a complete life are wise.

13. Natural truth is the foundation of life and the Universe. Religion is a rationalization for the darkness of the human mind that suppresses or misguides the healthy nature of life. No life can live apart from the natural truth. Religions are like the social fashions of a particular time; they are changeable, like clothing. Like clothing, too, they may also fit many people improperly.

According to natural reality, the healthiest of any species survives. The hallmarks of the new spiritual species of people come from their effort to live without violence, without drugs or alcohol, and without making trouble for themselves or others. Without impeding themselves in these ways, they are thus able to engage in spiritual learning and further the natural development of their lives.

Some of the Signers of the Original Declaration of Spiritual Independence:

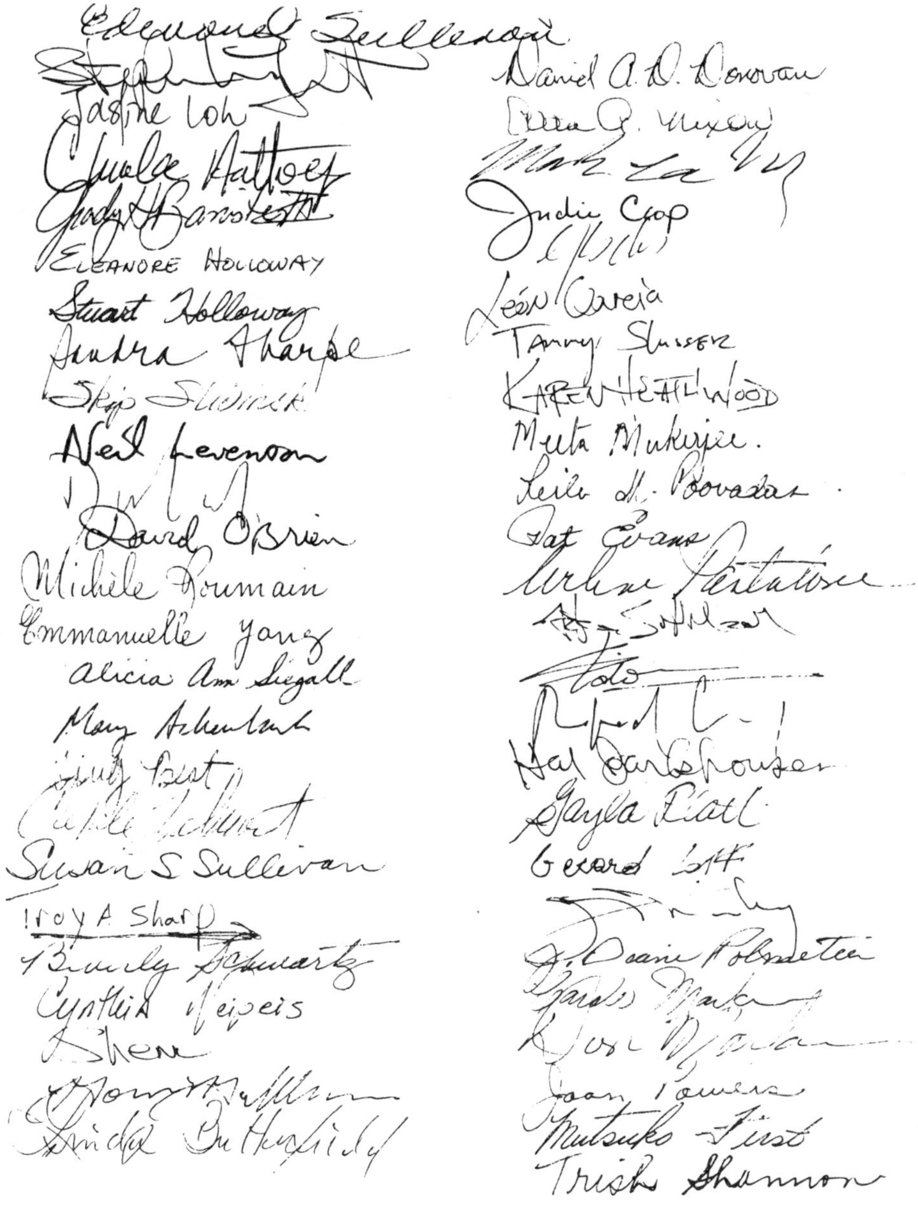

The above Declaration is made and supported by people of universal conscience and universal love who wish to renew themselves. Their spiritual position in nature is that of advanced lives. There is no salvation unless people save themselves. This Declaration of Spiritual Independence is the first step in a self-saving effort toward the spiritual awakening of all people.

The minimum effort required of all who wish to adopt this Declaration as their own is to refrain from violence, drugs, alcohol addiction, and making trouble for yourself or others. On the positive side, you should engage in broad spiritual learning that can lead to truthful attainment. This is not a commandment from God, this is the call of your own universal conscience. The real God lives inside of you and outside of you.

I welcome your deep contemplation of this Declaration. Should the high self obey the low self, or should the low self obey the high self? I remain your spiritual friend, whatever you conclude.

Personal Declaration
of
Spiritual Independence

By signing this Declaration, I hereby declare my spiritual independence and affirm my commitment to the spiritual development of my life. In keeping with this commitment, I will not engage in violent behavior of any kind, nor will I use drugs or become dependent upon alcohol. I will not make trouble for myself or other people, and I will be ever open to learning the universal spiritual truth.

Signed: _____

Witnessed: *The Universal Divine One*

You may frame and keep this certificate on your personal altar, carry it in your wallet or put it in any important place you wish to keep it.

INTERVIEW WITH
SHAMBHALA SUN

Halifax, Canada
October 14, 1994

Edited and supplemented for further clarity and deeper understanding.

I
Nature is the Highest Teacher

Shambhala Sun: In looking through your books, I see that you talk about Taoism. Actually, that is the only word in my vocabulary I feel I can use to describe what you write about. You write that the Taoist path does not rely upon religion or is one in which religion does not really play an important role. I am curious to know, then, if you don't call it a religion, what is the Taoist path?

Master Ni: Let me compare them for clarification. In the West, religion is like a social contract. Ancient Chinese culture does not regard spiritual teaching as a social contract. There is a big difference between Eastern and Western society. I admire the tolerance that has been practiced in the East for thousands of years, based on the foundation of Taoism as a culture. In the West, religion has always been an organized social force that imposes obligations upon people and interferes with their livelihood. Religions also separate people from one another. In my spiritual service, I teach tolerance and the natural viewpoint of life.

In the West you would call Buddhism a religion. In China, we would call it the teaching of Buddha. The East does not turn a spiritual teaching into a social force, thus people and families are not divided by different views. The majority of people in China accept Confucianism as the social order of their lives. Taoism, on the other hand, takes care of their health, while Buddhism covers the emotional side of everyday life. All other religions are considered different styles of worshipping the same Heaven. They do not affect the unity of the society.

After the communists took control of China, ideological differences intensified, and consequently affected personal and social relationships. Before this, China was a natural society whose long history of cultural integration encompassed great breadth and profundity, such as the integration of Buddhism with the teachings of Lao Tzu and Chuang Tzu. Islam, too, had become integrated among ancient Chinese customs. Some Chinese sects of Islam accepted and integrated the concepts of individual spiritual cultivation from Taoism and Buddhism. Chinese Catholics integrated their teachings with the teachings of Confucius, and in Taiwan, they now accept the old Chinese custom of ancestor worship, seeing that there is no conflict between the respect for family ancestors and the worship of God as spiritual ruler. Such natural integration occurred within a multi-cultural environment over several generations.

The long experience of Chinese people illustrates what is essential to human life. External formalities such as names and rituals are not essential. Just as I was not taught any prejudice, I wish to transplant the best of human spiritual achievement to the minds of this new generation so that they may focus on the deep harmony of the essence rather than superficial differences.

You know, human life did not suddenly appear on Earth; it has been here for millions of years, during which people experienced dark stages as well as brightness and progress. At times people have been smarter than at other times. Special individuals were inspired by their life experiences to reflect upon the fact that a subtle path exists. If we follow the subtle path, then we enjoy long, healthy lives. If we deviate too far from the natural truth of life, then we create trouble for ourselves and are bound to suffer the consequences.

The teaching of Tao comes from millions of years of human life experience. It is totally different than an externally established belief of any time. Particularly in the last 2,000 years, so many religions have been established as a form of cultural or political promotion. Nothing they teach seems related to natural life at all.

Shambhala Sun: My understanding is that in a religion like Buddhism, the forms and symbolism of the religion are what allow the teachings to be transmitted over time. Yet in Taoism, you talk about a subtle power or subtle energy that continues through generations and throughout time.

Master Ni: The teaching of Tao is not the subtle energy; the teaching of Tao is the recognition or understanding of the subtle power of nature. Nobody can own that power. It is through observation that you come to know the great reality that exists beyond physical force.

Shambhala Sun: In a civilization the size of China, there must be many people claiming to be authentic Taoist teachers. How does one go about discovering the Tao?

Master Ni: I believe you are interested in Buddhism and wish to compare it with the teaching of the Way, so let me use that as an example. Today, what is called Buddhism is very different from the actual teaching of Sakyamuni. Historical records show that the two teachings are very different. What happened is, during each generation, new leaders superimposed conventional images on their own new ideas to develop new codes of behavior or new social fashions. Thus, the new teaching was not at all related to what the Buddha taught. Actually, Buddhism today goes against almost everything Sakyamuni taught. I don't know if you are aware of that or not.

Sakyamuni was a kind-hearted individual who reflected on the life condition of people of his time. At that time, Brahmanism was very popular. If you were born into a low class or a slave family, you could not change it. For example, you could not marry into another class, because the Brahman priests said that was your *karma*, and that was God's decision. If you were reborn into a lower or inferior family or class, it was predestined as a sort of punishment that you deserved.

Buddha thought that the whole thing was ridiculous. He did not continue the theories of *karma* or reincarnation. So he established his theory about the most important influences upon human life, which he called conditions. Buddha thought that anything and everything that exists is present only because of a certain group of conditions.

Shambhala Sun: I understand what you mean.

Master Ni: Good. So you can see that he did not continue the conventional social ideology of his time. He was a revolutionary.

Long after he died, around 500 years later, new leaders came to use him as a spiritual image. They put the theories of *karma* and reincarnation back together as a new religion and created a new form of Buddhism that was quite different from what Sakyamuni taught. Mahayana Buddhism is basically Brahmanism revived in a new form. That was interesting, because what Buddha said was that religion and idol worship were the wrong path. But people came back to play the same game, with him as the object of worship, the new God who is able to take care of all your troubles.

When we talk about the teaching of Tao, we are speaking of a totally natural reality. Tolerance is the essence of personal and social progress. The teaching of Tao has no connection with any ideological struggles or religious attitudes.

II
Seeing the Truth
is the Result of Personal Growth

Shambhala Sun: So then, how are the teachings of the Tao transmitted and communicated over time? Do they pass through individuals or through a set of practices?

My understanding is that, and please correct me if I am wrong, much of philosophical Taoism is rooted in the teachings of Lao Tzu, Chuang Tzu, and to a certain extent the I Ching.

Master Ni: Around 12,000 to 20,000 years ago, there was a sage called Fu Shi. He was a developed person, who continued the ancient learning and worked to develop the system we call the *I Ching.*

Lao Tzu did not initiate Taoism. He was a historian and librarian who kept the cultural records for the royal court of the Chou dynasty, thus he had the opportunity to learn what the ancients had left behind. He studied this material, and he also had his own teachers. He compiled his learning into the *Tao Teh Ching* and started teaching what he called the Indescribable Way. However, what can be described with words is not really what he wished to communicate, because that is the ordinary level that anyone can find in everyday life. What he called the Way exists behind regularly observed general phenomenon and is more subtle. That subtle trace cannot be defined in the same way as the reality that is visible, but it can be called "the Way." That was how he described the natural universal reality. He also used the words "the Way" to illustrate the *I Ching.*

All things that can be observed are manifest, but behind the manifest exists what is unmanifest. Do you remember the philosophy or principle of *yin* and *yang?* The development of this Universe comes from those two spheres, the manifest sphere and the unmanifest sphere, embracing each other. This dynamic relativity is the reality of the Universe.

Shambhala Sun: Is the teaching of balance, then, the basis of the teachings of Tao?

Master Ni: There are many important applications and ways to understand *yin* and *yang.* A simple description, as you know, is that they are two forces that balance each other. Therefore, the best way to conduct one's life is to not become overly positive or aggressive, nor overly passive. In other words, a person must find balance. This is the constant, endless path of universal life.

Shambhala Sun: To return to my earlier question, how are the teachings of the Tao transmitted through time, and how do they continue to exist today? How is it that you have the opportunity to present these teachings

Master Ni: The Universal Way is not a monastically organized religion, whereby each generation passes it down through individual teachers or family members. The teaching of the Universal Way happens naturally. In each society, some individuals have a natural drive to know more about what is behind the surface of life. Those people develop themselves or look for teachers who can help them to develop further. However, someone might follow a teacher for decades and still not know the truth. Someone else, however, may have already found the answer and wish to find someone of deep understanding to verify it. In a very short time, this person's thoughts and understanding would be confirmed by the teacher or corrected.

Sometimes we use the term "attaining Tao" to describe one's spiritual growth. Attaining Tao is similar to self-enlightenment in some ways, but the question "What is the self?" is the one that leads to discovering the depth of life. Natural enlightenment may help you understand more about life and its troubles. Sometimes you only understand a little bit more, because your enlightenment is only through the mouth and tongue. If you are involved with a type of ideology that can be exhibited or publicized, it cannot be considered real enlightenment.

Natural enlightenment comes from asking ourselves questions such as: Why are we here? Why do people become aggressive? Why do human tendencies change back and forth? Why, during certain times, is there a dominating force that obstructs the natural progress of society? Why have there been so few really enlightened individuals in human history? Why are there so many who rigidly follow somebody's thought even without understanding clearly what they are following?

The transmission of Tao is individual. It is not an organized ideology that can be passed down, except for the self-development arts, which need to be passed down from generation to generation so they will not be lost.

We can no longer trace the early stages of how these arts were passed down. Developed individuals view all of nature as their own lives, thus personal names were not important. The later stages of the transmission of Tao can be traced because they were passed through certain families or lineages of teachers.

Shambhala Sun: Are you saying that somebody could discover the teachings of the Tao in their life, and only call it the Tao afterward?

Master Ni: All people have the capability to discover the Tao in their lives, if they pursue it.

At different times and in different places, the Way has been given different names, compared to the strongly defined terms of an organized religion. The teaching of the Way developed sort of like a random culture. The Way is derived from the personal development of special individuals, who live not as priests, but as ordinary people. Priests are people who make religion their profession, so they need to gather social support. If you attain the Way, your purpose is not to make money out of it, and there is no social recognition for it. Wisdom is the attainment. Truly achieved people are not proud, because all they have achieved is simply the personal discovery of the natural spiritual source or origin of life. This achievement provides the possibility for the spiritual survival of individual life, but it is totally different from the idealized afterlife of socially organized religions.

When the culture of India moved North, it motivated the establishment of shamanistic Taoism which still exists in China today and is not really related to my teaching.

Shambhala Sun: So there is a folk or shamanistic religion called Taoism amongst the Chinese?

Master Ni: Yes, but it is not related to Lao Tzu's teaching, although they respect Lao Tzu as their divinity. When you read Lao Tzu's teaching, you can see that he had no intention of establishing any type of religious worship.

Shambhala Sun: What do you think about other religions?

Master Ni: There is a profound difference in the value of religious teaching and natural teaching. Natural teaching comes from an individual's own self-reflection. Teachers of natural truth may write a book or conduct a public service, but they do not insist upon anything. They have no reason to assemble a congregation or mislead people.

Each era has its own expression. No one fashion can be popular always. We consider it spiritually unvirtuous to impose a 2,000 year old social design on people's lives. We need to be open to human growth, realizing that once a religion becomes dominant and over-established, it impedes the growth of future generations. Openness is a totally different approach than the dogmatic allegiance required by most religions. Religions rarely have anything to do with the deep natural truth, they are only expressions of the mental stage of people at one time, not of all times. Sometimes people might have the chance to glimpse the truth, but they are usually too controlled by the church to ever pursue that glimpse very far. It is not correct to establish and then impose one's preference upon all people for all times.

III
The Natural Truth
is the Fountain of True Wisdom

Shambhala Sun: I am sure there were periods in China's history when many people, or a good number of people, appreciated the approach to life which you just talked about. How could they avoid not transmitting the truths and ways of living in accordance with the Tao to their children, through the schools, through politics and through their social systems? If you discover something that seems to be genuine and true, how can you not?

Master Ni: It is a matter of non-insistence. I was never told that I must be exactly the same as my parents. They didn't make a good approach to life into a law, because they knew that above all laws is the unchangeable subtle law. Human law and human custom are always adaptable; they change with each new understanding and situation of life. The attitude of the Way is to allow things to change in a correct manner, in a positive way.

Shambhala Sun: What about personal practices?

Master Ni: There are many personal practices that are great treasures of human spiritual development. We do not assign personal authority over these practices to any individual, but we do know the value of passing it to the right person at the right time. You are sincere and wish to learn more about this. Perhaps you do not realize that your education and the society you were born in have formed you in a certain way, so this new understanding may seem out of reach. My teaching at this time is very valuable to people of a natural mind. I do not insist upon an organized, religious way. I encourage people to find the truth in their own way. All the teaching I have given and will give can be self-proven. It represents the highest attainment of the human mind over thousands of years.

Shambhala Sun: How do you feel about North American society today and its capacity to come to terms with or to recognize the truth of the Tao?

Master Ni: I teach not only in the United States but throughout the whole world, particularly in areas such as Europe and the South Pacific, including Australia and New Zealand. Before I taught in the Western hemisphere I taught in the Orient. During the last 20 years, my focus has been on the English speaking world, including English-speaking Chinese societies such as Singapore. Some of them have been greatly benefitted by my restating the ancient Chinese teachings in my simple and sometimes clumsy English.

Eastern people have an Eastern mentality, Western people have a Western mentality, and Middle Eastern people have a Middle Eastern mentality. It is their mentality which forms their different religions. Their spiritual essence, however, is the same.

For example, Buddhism might be considered a passive type of mentality, whereas Islam could be interpreted as overly aggressive. Yet I cannot say that Muslims are really more aggressive than the Christian missionaries who knock on the doors of all continents. Christians, too, think that all non-believers are infidels. In both cases, this unhealthy merger of ignorance with arrogance has resulted in the wholesale slaughter of untold numbers of innocent human beings.

You might wonder what type of mentality is best. The human mind has multiple functions: sometimes you need to be positive, but at other times you need to be opposing. Sometimes you need to be very active, but at a different time or place, you need to be inactive. In other words, no single type of mentality is superior; all are suitable at different times and places.

Truly developed people appreciate all healthy functions of the mind, thus they keep their balance and can rise above so-called religious conflict. Truthfully, religions are rationalized expressions of different mentalities. That is my evaluation, after a lifetime of study and observation.

My work is to put East and West together to appreciate, complement and supplement each other, because no single type of mentality is inherently higher than the others. All people need flexibility.

A German psychologist named Carl Jung, and his friend Richard Wilhelm, translated the *I Ching,* which was a start at putting East and West together. After them, Arnold Joseph Toynbee of Great Britain wrote several important books about world culture, then Joseph Needham also made an effort to bring East and West closer through his fine scholarship and writings.

Shambhala Sun: In your experience, what religion represents the rationalized mentality of North America?

Master Ni: Christianity is still the main expression of Western society. We need to know what should be appreciated and what should be forsaken. We need to see what is spiritually backward and unfit in all religions. This requires total understanding.

On one hand, people's intellectual strength is more advanced than it was 2,000 years ago, but on the other hand, what is valuable still deserves appreciation. For example, around 12,000 to 20,000 years ago when Fu Shi discovered the *I Ching* system, that was the descriptive cosmology of his time. Generations have proven that reality of so long ago to still be true today. The most valuable discovery made by Fu Shi was the subtle energy that makes communication possible between the conscious and the subconscious mind, and between people's own mental projections and the corresponding reflection of external reality. How can this be so? Because there is a universal subtle energy which is the subtle connection among all people and all things.

According to Biblical scholars, the span from the day that God created the world through the time of Noah and the flood, up until today, has only been around 12,000 years. Some people still insist that this is true rather than metaphoric. I don't bother about such childish things, because people's perception and understanding depend on their own level of development, which you cannot change by external force. But anyone who is aggressive about imposing their understanding on others expresses something other than spiritual health.

I think that in North America, many fine young people like yourself are facing a time of religious confusion. It is not a matter of who is right or wrong, it is a matter of seeing that different mentalities express themselves differently and create ideologies and rituals that reinforce their mentality. That is the bottom line. The differences are essentially of no importance whatsoever.

Shambhala Sun: I agree.

Master Ni: This is an important time for all of us. No matter what our forerunners have given us, this is a new time. It is not a time to reinforce our separateness. Instead, I wish to work out a new bright way: the Universal Way. I don't feel happy about any religion coming from East to West if it makes young people walk away from a normal way of life and conduct their lives out of an immature wish to be different from their society. Unfortunately, Western teachings really don't provide the younger generation with a good way to develop themselves and to express their spiritual differences. So far, better health is the only goal they seem to have in common, and that is certainly a positive beginning.

Some people have attained a higher understanding and no longer insist upon past conventions, but respect the essence of all traditions. This is what I have done, and this is why I call the Universal Way a trans-religion. It insists upon no religion, but takes a balanced spiritual attitude toward all spiritual paths. This is my message.

Science makes many religious people feel threatened, and they try to suppress facts about the history of the Earth and the heavenly bodies. Thus, those people who represent the intellectual mind go one way, and religious people who insist on what their ancestors believed go another way, considering any advance in human knowledge as hostile toward their way of life. I think it is time for these two camps to recognize each other. They are actually not so different, because the humanistic motivation of the advanced sciences and the advanced spiritual sciences should be the same. Both are looking for the truth inside and outside of the world.

If a religion is truthful, people should face the facts and learn to respect the natural truth of life. Then maybe the mind and the spirit can find a way to meet each other. This is the Universal Way.

IV
The Truth Needs to be Conveyed Accurately

Shambhala Sun: One hopes the day will come when different societies and religions can communicate with each other. At that point, they would need a language or a common experience in order to create a harmonious society.

Master Ni: I offer my teaching of the Universal Way because I feel it can provide such a bridge.

Religion can also find a counterpart in psychology, particularly through Buddhism, which recognizes that the fictitious nature of all religions originate in the mind. For instance, Western religions believe that God created the world, but God is a self-recognition of the human soul projected onto the memory or image of the father of a family or chieftain of a tribe.

The most recent studies in physics are finding exactly what the *I Ching* described thousands of years ago. I welcome all of you to examine the *I Ching* and learn the relationship between the pure natural mind and the subtle energy of nature. The *I Ching* is a paradigm for universal life that was discovered around 12,000 years ago. What can we add to that today?

Shambhala Sun: So the I Ching *is the paradigm of the universe?*

Master Ni: It presents the depth of the unspoiled intuition of the natural mind. It might not seem very different from today's discoveries in the realm of physics, but the approach is totally different. Whether you use mathematics or other academic or experimental disciplines, the *I Ching* includes the basic principles of those observations, but it also includes the important role of the intuitive mind. Whereas science is considered to be the result or the fruit of the intellectual mind, ancient discoveries were the fruit of the intuitive mind.

The reality of spirituality is no different today than it ever was. Even if you are a scientist, your greatest discovery is not merely the result of the intellectual mind. When you relax, the intuitive function of mind helps you find the solution you wish to discover. So all scientists and inventors, particularly in the last 200 to 300 years, have not made their achievements with their intellectual minds alone. The intuitive mind intervened to help the discovery or achievement.

All functions of a healthy mind should be respected. Conventionally, the intuitive mind has been called God and the intellectual mind Satan. This represents spiritual undevelopment and religious nonsense. I teach the integralness of the two.

People formerly exalted only religious leaders or hermits as godly, but you can find God in Thomas Jefferson, Thomas Edison, Abraham Lincoln, Albert Einstein, Alexander Graham Bell and many other remarkable people who made positive contributions in all spheres of life. Anyone who makes a worthwhile contribution with humanistic intentions should be regarded as expressing godly energy. Many rulers or religious leaders throughout history did very little to further benefit the world.

My teaching is called the Universal Society of the Integral Way, or the Universal Way for short. It teaches the Integral Way of Life, which is to put body, mind and soul together. I respect advanced scientists who make a real contribution. I consider myself a researcher of the science of natural life, and my achievement has been attained through ancient spiritual methods that were proven by countless achieved beings for thousands of years. This is what I can offer: proof of subtle energy. It can be found only when you are peaceful.

Shambhala Sun: When you say subtle energy, is that the Tao?

Master Ni: It is close. Tao is just a term. For example, your question was first a thought, then a sound, but before it was even a thought or a sound, it was something subtle. You did not feel its existence, but at the time you vocalized it through your body, it became a vibration from the inside out. That subtle vibration is the foundation of the high mind. That subtle vibration is the foundation of the high Universe.

I would like to give you an example of the responsive spirit inside yourself. If you are not egotistical or ideological, you have a peaceful mind, and when you face a situation, you either need to look into yourself or find somebody to help you find a practical solution. You don't need to go far away, and it is not necessary to kneel down and yell to God for help. Your mind can produce the answer as thoughts or inspiration. You think it is God who comes around to you, but it is only the high mind guiding the low mind.

In our practice, we simply sit down quietly and use a form of divination, such as the *I Ching*, which always gives an accurate answer. If you talk about God as the ruler, there is none existing in nature. But there is Tao, the subtle energy and subtle connection among all things. Tao is the high truth.

If you want proof of the existence of the subtle energy that is everywhere, you can find its response to your mind at any time. This subtle reality can prove the divine nature within you and also the divine nature outside of you. Spiritual truth is not a matter of overly exalting an individual image as God. Spiritual truth is integral; it includes you and me and all others. Because it is subtle, you must be very peaceful to notice it, because only then can your mind possess or at least effectively communicate or transmit the application of subtle universal energy.

Shambhala Sun: Then at the core of the teachings that you share with people and that have been transmitted to you from your parents and teachers is the notion of subtle energy?

Master Ni: It is not a notion, it is real. Buddhist friends would say that the Universe is a void. I say that there is subtle energy everywhere. It is responsive and reflective like a mirror: if you smile to the subtle reality of the Universe, it smiles back. If you make a face at it, it makes the same face back, because it is a subtle responsive substance. Being able to evoke a good subtle response is what the ancients called "spiritual." They sensed that the Universe is like an individual being. That is a truthful way to describe it, as a corresponding, responsive and reciprocal effect. When you treat someone well, that is equal to smiling at the Universe. When you treat someone poorly, that equals you treating the Universe badly. I call this the law of correspondence. However you project your life energy, the Universe reflects it back to you.

I have written a book called *Tao, the Subtle Universal Law* which you can read to learn more about this. My books, the *Key to Good Fortune* and the *Book of Changes and the Unchanging Truth* also discuss it in more detail. All of my books can help you recognize the subtle law in your life.

Universal reality is subtle. It is the law of the Universe itself. We are children of the Universe. In the Universe, the most valued energy is the most effective, responsive energy. Here we are, looking to the subtle energy just like young children always turn to their parents for help. In some situations, you can expect help from your physical parents, but not always, because they may live too far away or may have already passed away. However, you can always find help from the real source of life, the subtle sphere of universal energy, which is the origin of the physical Universe and of us.

Shambhala Sun: So living in harmony with the Tao would be the way to connect with the subtle energy of the universe?

Master Ni: That is right. By living quietly with our subtle energy, we discover that the Universe is inside of us and outside of us. If everything we do is in accordance with the subtle law, things go smoothly. However, once we do or say things that deviate from the subtle law, trouble comes. The subtle law cannot be written, only your own growth helps you attain harmony with it. My parents would personify it as the Universal Mother.

V
The Subtle Truth Has No Form:
The Intellectual Mind Has Form

Shambhala Sun: I understand some of what you are saying, but it is hard for me not to think of Taoism as a form of spirituality or as a spiritual path. When I look at you and your life, and I look at the books that you have written and some of your teachings, I cannot help but think that you are offering a way of life.

Master Ni: Yes, it is the universal spiritual path which is trans-religional. It covers all the religions. If we insist to serve as a religion, then we are serving people differently. To express the difference, I would say that although we have our own spiritual symbols, they carry a different and deep meaning. It is not a worshipping religion. If we accept the word "religion," we are the religion of natural balanced life. It is the religion of spiritual self-development of all people. It is the religion of spiritual self-cultivation of all individuals. It is the religion of universal oneness, and it is the religion of the re-union of universal divinity and people. We have formed the Universal Society of the Integral Way by volunteer helpers working together to make this teaching more effective.

I would say the reason that you view my teaching as a spiritual path is that there are so many types of teaching today, yet my teaching and my voice are different, practical and down to earth. Certainly, the people around me have formalized a way of life, but that is not a requirement in my teaching, although it can have a good function in modern times. If the service I offer is not effective, useful, and truthful, why should I do it? There is no personal gain in it for me, but I gain the Universe. I do not acquire social power or gather people under my control to satisfy my ego or ambition. I work because I love all young people. I am still a young person, so I wish to work together with all of you.

Since I teach spiritual growth, spiritual development and spirituality, it is correct to call the Universal Way a spiritual path, but not a religion. Yet it is much more than just a spiritual path. Deeply, it is still not correct to see the Universal Way as another spiritual path.

The difference between the Universal Way and religions lies in the difference between the maturity of human attainment and old customs that were established at an early stage of human development. An immature mind looks for support, not growth. If you look to religion for spiritual maturity, you are knocking on the wrong door. It is similar to a widower with a baby knocking on the door of a nunnery to find someone to breastfeed the baby. No religion offers maturity. Maturity is attained through life experience, but experience is sometimes very costly. So you can combine your life experience with your knowledge of religions and further, of the Universal Way. You are encouraged to attain maturity and rise above all religions. The Universal Way assists the maturity of human nature through the achievement and development of all generations as the foundation for further human development. This is why I call it the Universal Way.

I suggest that students read my upcoming book *New Physics: Gateway to Tao* in which I discuss the maturity of the mind and the truthful attainment of a meditative life. I don't want the masses to continually be misguided. According to the ancient spiritually developed ones, maturity is not for sale, but is a reward to excellent students whose good minds are open to high teachings.

No individual's wisdom can be recognized as the wisdom of the Universe, but together we can discover the same universal truth as the ancient developed ones did. Sharing our understanding of universal truth will make us happy. All spiritual truth is contained in all individuals. All people of deep appreciation can come together to improve the world and fulfill the Universal Integral Way.

Shambhala Sun: I'm not comfortable with religion in general, and I think that many other people are not, but they pursue a religious path because they sense that at the heart of religion there is some kind of genuine insight into subtle energy or maybe into how life works. I think that for some people, it is difficult to separate social conventions from actual practice in the religion. In your teachings, I don't know how else to phrase it, but there seems to be a desire not to talk about it as a religion, and I appreciate that. I also think that there are a lot of people who are interested in that approach to life, because they are not interested in all of the baggage that comes with religion. Yet, many people think that they must accept that baggage in order to get to the heart of what the religion has to offer.

Master Ni: Yes, some of the misleading aspects of human culture are over emphasized. This has become a burden for the younger generation, because it needs to spend decades unlearning things that were deeply instilled in their minds, and they still do not find the truth. If they come to enjoy the truthful discovery, they can live as simply and as happily as I.

Shambhala Sun: Are you saying there are too many options available?

Master Ni: There are not only too many good things available, there are also too many bad things. It is similar to the new politics: the American government sets up one program and then another. They spend a lot of energy to pass a bill to set up an expensive program, then a year later they discover that the program is no good. Thus, they need to pass another bill, and go through another big expense to fix this program. This continues on and on until they have built up a huge national debt, but they have not achieved anything at all.

Culturally, it is the same thing. We talk about having a different ideology or different life path, but practically, what really serves life? Life is so simple and natural, you don't need to add anything to it to give it value. I would rather talk about a good way to live than make a religion out of something. I don't consider vegetarianism as the holy way to eat, because people of different ages who do different types of work need different types of diet. On the other hand, people in the Middle East say that you can only eat beef and not swine, all for a holy reason. The truth is that good food of any kind, when it is needed, is holy. Not out of any holy or religious reason can war ever be justified, except for the uprightness of defending oneself against aggression. Specific customs sometimes lack a truthful background and are really groundless. This is why it is better for us to be open to all great things, and to see which are applicable and which are not applicable.

My teaching is like a school in which no student must be enrolled for a lifetime. They come to learn from me and make use of the knowledge in their lives, but they not are required to say, "This is the only truth."

From ancient times until now, the Universal Way has been taught as a broad form of universal spiritual education, not a narrow religious teaching.

Why don't I recommend religion to young friends? Because there are two kinds of people who fool you: preachers and politicians.

Most people don't have a deep understanding of life, and religious leaders and politicians could at least conduct themselves earnestly and with good conscience, but they usually do not. Their conduct has created a false culture in the world and has never produced any benefit for other people. The only benefit they have ever produced has been for themselves alone. I consider this a con business. It is not truthful, because spiritual reality is in you and in everybody. You only need to show people the correct way of life and how to think. No decent person should invent a fiction and make other people conform to it. Religion should encourage people to attain spiritual development, but instead they block it. Once you become their customer, your own growth is powerfully limited.

Shambhala Sun: So you think that religion inhibits spiritual growth?

Master Ni: Definitely.   Real life experience is what makes people grow, not religion.   Religion is rooted in the shortcomings of human nature.   Its strength comes from the human weakness of needing something or someone to rely on.

The Universal Way encourages people to search for the truth, goodness and power of character as their own personal spiritual development. There is no limit to your personal development; it is only teachings that are limited. How much any teaching can offer is determined by the attainment of those before you. Development is for yourself and the people of future generations.

The Universal Way encourages you to attain spiritual independence. It does not mean that once you become my student you should be less than I am. If you are my student, you are my future further developed spiritual life.

The Universal Way encourages people to attain spiritual freedom. When you learn the Universal Way, you do not exchange your spiritual freedom for any temporary psychological support. People come to me because they wish to attain their spiritual freedom.

These are things that no religion can offer you. Independence means to depend upon oneself for learning and achievement. The goal of spiritual learning is to not become dependent upon someone else. Freedom means no limitation. This is what the Universe offers you. This is why this path is called the Universal Way.

Shambhala Sun: I have a question which is in some way related. In North America and other parts of the world today, there is tremendous confusion about what is commonly called gender roles and confusion about the relationship between man and woman. People have a difficult time in their relationships with the opposite sex or the same sex. It is true that people have always had difficulty in their relationships, but now there is more ambiguity or confusion about how these relationships should unfold.

Master Ni: The following chart comes from my personal understanding and knowledge of human health. It does not take a statistical approach.

Sexual Lifestyle	"A" means good for life
1. Celibacy practiced through external self-discipline and internal sublimation	AAA
2. Celibacy artlessly practiced for a supposed spiritual purpose by those who know nothing of the art of sublimation	
3. Celibacy practiced for reasons of health such as during recovery or just general weakness	A
4. Celibacy practiced despite a healthy sexual function, not because of impotence or frigidity; person lives an otherwise ordinary life	
5. A well-matched heterosexual life	AAA
6. A less well-matched heterosexual life	A
7. A random heterosexual life	
8. A well-matched non-heterosexual consistent relationship for years similar to ordinary marriage or long term relationship	A
9. Non-heterosexual disciplined sex for self-adjustment	
10. A random non-heterosexual life	

Explanation of chart:

1.   Artful sublimation is a serious path of spiritual cultivation. Few people have achieved it, but their achievement has been high and real, without the need for physical union. In general, changing the focus of life to concentrate on achieving life goals, projects or other pursuits will decrease one's sexual pressure. The high level *chi*

kung known as internal alchemy requires sexual temperance or celibacy.

2. If your mind is strong enough, this is a way to save trouble, but it is not completely healthy because it is physically very depressing.

3. This is suitable when practiced with self-awareness or guidance from a competent individual.

4. If you are physically strong, your emotions will tend to be violent or jealous under these conditions. The result would be psychological subnormalcy.

5. In this lifestyle, there is harmony between *yin* and *yang* with natural spiritual benefit.

6. Although there is still a physical exchange, the union is not complete in such a relationship.

7. Like overeating or starving, this approach is a temporary situation to the emotional difficulty of managing sexual energy.

8. Some males are born feminine inside because the womb of the mother did not provide them with enough masculine energy to deal emotionally with the difficulties of life. There are physical, psychological or practical reasons for them to stay together as a couple.

9. This is less trouble for women than for men, but it is still not encouraged because there is no exchange between two types of energy. Nevertheless, it may save you from having psychological difficulty.

10. This causes too much harm to men. It depletes the *yang* energy which affects the strength of the immune system. It represents physical unusualness or psychological confusion.

Individual sexual exploration should place health and morality above sexual freedom and ignorance.

Sexual attitudes are a matter of personal growth. Selectiveness is the key to successful sexual practice. Periodic celibacy is also beneficial for most people for health and spiritual reasons. If you wish to know more about this subject, you may study my elucidation of the *I Ching*. One section consists of general guidance, and the other is divination for specific situations.

People's minds are usually able to reflect a matter accurately. If a matter is important to you, but there is no accurate knowledge of any sort, you may use the *I Ching* to help your understanding.

VI
The Truth of Life Presents Health

Shambhala Sun: I have always been interested in the close relationship between spiritual practice and medical treatment. It seems that followers or teachers or practitioners of the Tao, people like yourself, always seems to have a strong association with medical or nutritional practice. The teachings always seem to include recommendations about diet, lifestyle, exercise, sexual manners, etc. and the ancient Taoist masters are often known to have had a great understanding of how the body works and about emotional attunement. Is that an exaggeration?

Master Ni: No, but attainment is individual. We are not a closed-end religion; we are an open-end life path. Natural, integral spiritual practices and Chinese medicine are related systems of knowledge. Modern medicine is based upon anatomy and biochemistry. In contrast, integral medicine is based upon the spiritual development of the practitioners who take care of the health of others and themselves.

The matter of life, particularly human life, is not merely a physical matter; people have a non-material mind, emotion and spirit. That level is not touched by modern medicine, which is incomplete. Complete medicine treats life as a whole, it treats the individual as a whole; it does not rely solely on technology to treat people like soulless machines.

What you asked about is a very important question that needs to be examined with an open mind. Spiritual cultivation is not a matter of sitting all day long, stewing over your psychological problems. Realistic spiritual development sharpens your internal senses. People who engage in spiritual cultivation in a correct manner, such as living quietly, know dangers beforehand and can thus avoid them if at all possible. They are able to know trouble and sickness before they happen, and can thus reduce the seriousness of disease or perhaps avoid it altogether. They even have a stronger immune system that can both protect and cure them. This is why they live long, healthy and happy lives.

When some people who have achieved themselves leave their bodies, it means that it is the right time for their souls to go, before their physical shell fails them. It is a natural reality of life that all people have a time to come and a time to go. What happens in modern medicine, however, is that doctors are not educated to know that life is natural. A suitable amount of intervention can be helpful, but overly intervening in the body's natural processes not only does not help, but can actually create more difficulty for the patient.

The worst thing a doctor can do is disrespect a living or dying body. For example, around 20 years ago, when I was still in the Orient, I had a spiritual friend who was older than myself and who had practiced Pure Land Buddhism for over 40 years. He lived a day away from me by train. For a long time, he prepared to have a painless death. Then, when he was 93 years old, he knew that he needed to go. He sat crosslegged and gently vibrated the word *Amitabha* in Chinese. He was preparing for his soul to leave. However, someone phoned his son, a physician, who rushed over from the hospital and forced the father out of the lotus position in which he was seated. He did not understand that to be able to sit in such a posture was one of his father's lifetime attainments. The son, who was a doctor himself, sent his father to the hospital and used all kinds of modern advanced techniques to prevent his death. In his ignorance, he just did not know to leave his dying father alone; his modern techniques only interfered with the dying life that was ready for its soul to ascend. I felt great sorrow for the destructive effects of this young man's shallow education on his father's ascending soul. He obviously thought that his training encompassed the truth of human life. I do not blame the son's natural emotion at the time of his father's passing, but I do say that his medical education was sadly incomplete.

Let me give you another, more positive, example. There was a wealthy Chinese man whose fortune was not the result of exploiting laborers, as Karl Marx would have liked to imagine. The majority of wealthy Chinese people had become rich through generations of hard work, good means of accumulation and effective systems of management, despite communist propaganda to the contrary. Mr. Kou, an old style capitalist from China, had owned a textile factory before becoming a refugee in 1949 when communism destroyed the old natural society and turned China into a den of beasts.

Mr. Kou first fled to Brazil with his family of five sons and one daughter. He understood life and the meaning of wealth after experiencing the ravages of war, and he had a strong interest in the learning the Way. He was not active in business after going abroad because his sons took care of that. Then he moved to the United States.

Several years before I moved to the United States, Mr. Kou visited me when I was teaching. His other way of passing time was to sit in the Las Vegas casinos to do some small gambling. Because my main service is treating people with traditional Chinese medicine, I started traveling around the world for spiritual service and to treat patients.

One day about seven years ago he came to see me with his two sons to relate his physical situation. He was perfectly alright, but for six months he did not need to eat food any more. During that time, he only drank some pure water. He was quite spiritual and asked my instruction because he had already decided to leave his body. I carefully gave him instructions for his ascension, which were to keep the conscious mind undisturbed and clear in order for the disassembly between the body and the soul to be peaceful. There should be no type of intervention, and one should remember that the spiritual focus is upward. One's focus should not be downward in any way, and to help that, a person's worldly responsibilities should be transferred long before that day. The preferable hour to go is between the hours of midnight and high noon when the sun is in its rising cycle, because souls were originally produced by the sun's rays. Then we said farewell.

Several months later, after our meeting, I received a call telling me that my old friend had ascended. The family had no doubt about his ascension. He had clearly instructed his family what to do on that day. If he had been put in a hospital, it would have been a disaster. His two sons stayed in the room with him. For the first several nights, they were attentive, which affected the father's peace of mind, but eventually the two young men became tired and fell asleep. Then Mr. Kou launched his "missile," his soul quietly ascending into the sky without anyone noticing. His body had no trace of a struggle or suffering; he was just like a healthy man sleeping. In fact, his family was so sure he was in sleeping meditation that they hated to cremate him, expecting him to wake up as usual. After six days or so, they became afraid of the pressure from their neighbors, and they obeyed the father's bidding, which was to burn his body.

I hope these stories can help you understand why I feel that most young people who wish to become involved with complete healing have a spiritual mission.

It has been proven that religion, politics and modern technology do not have all the answers to the world's problems. In ancient times, people had fewer psychological problems because society was more natural. They were able to attain what was so easy to attain: a natural life. If one person worked, the whole family could be fed. It is not like today, when you need to go through many complicated learning processes, and then you still do not know the correct way to fulfill your life.

The ancients had a chance to carefully observe and objectively experience the internal truth of life. The internal truth of life is that each individual contains numerous spiritual entities. Through biochemistry or anatomy, these entities can never be found; it takes spiritual cultivation to verify their existence. Doctors are among the first ones who should develop themselves spiritually; otherwise, they are students of nothing more than books, animals and dead people. For example, modern psychologists, learn from mice. However, understanding mice is different than understanding humans, but modern research has established that different way of learning.

I encourage young doctors in modern science and modern medicine who wish to attain a new breakthrough to look for it in the right place. It will not be found under the lenses of their microscopes, but through personal spiritual cultivation. This is the only way to discover the unique truth that each individual is composed of numerous spiritual entities.

You might ask me, is this provable? Yes; I hold the formula to prove it. You might ask me, then why don't you give people that formula? Well, I do tell people, but the reason that I don't tell everyone is because such things can only be given as a response to sincere seekers. This knowledge is not something I can make a show out of. Spiritual things are so subtle that only through your own experience can you verify their solid truth. It is not a matter of physics, it is a matter of the depth of physics.

Once you discover the truth that you have internal spirits, then you will also know the existence of other natural spirits, and you will know for yourself if there is a God or not.

If the scientists who dominate modern medicine would like to make a new scientific breakthrough and experience the complete truth for themselves, I invite them to learn the practical process of proving human spirituality. I may not know the external style in which they describe reality, but I do know the internal reality of life that is spiritual. I can teach people how to find the truth, so that they can work to effectively change the culture in which we live. Before modern medicine can be expected to change, its practitioners need to discover the subtle truth that is not as rigid as what is in their textbooks. The vitality of human nature is not composed exactly the way modern physics says it is. *Chi*, the spiritual entity or entities of physical life, has numerous transformations, and because it is so subtle, you are unable to see it. Yet, it still can be experienced by a spiritual individual.

If this process was offered to the world, particularly to leading scientists, and if they earnestly, humbly and sincerely became students of natural spiritual truth, the universal way, the integral way of life, I would be very hopeful for the future of the world. In any case, I will continue to teach my friends so that they can know the truth. However, I will never encourage them to formulate fixed attitudes about it. Attacking the world is wrong.

VII
The Universe Serves Its Own Health

Shambhala Sun: Going back to a previous question, how or why do Taoist teachers and followers of Tao seem to have a very strong interest in and sensitivity to physical health and physical well-being? It is unusual, looking at other spiritual traditions - and forgive me for classifying Taoism as a spiritual tradition. In fact, it is very rare to encounter any sensitivity to physical health or practices or treatments involved in cultivating or maintaining physical health in other spiritual traditions. I have always been curious to know why that might be. What is it about the Tao that fosters this?

Master Ni: Most religions tend to overlook the physical foundation of life. We don't think that way; we respect life in its entirety. We think that human life is the highest form of natural evolution. The universal existence was not created by any human ancestor, even if religious mythology says so. It started long ago, before humans ever appeared on the earth. Humans are latecomers. They are the fruit of universal development. You can find the true God in people.

You could say that humans are gods of the natural world, because through spiritual practice we can discover three important things about natural life: one, the material foundation of life does not last forever; two, the human soul must leave the failing body; three, the human character or personality is what the soul carries with it and is the foundation of the soul itself. For example, if a person died many years ago, he or she may come back through a medium, and in this communication, their personality, emotion etc., are still the same.

Practicing spiritual cultivation and conducting your personal life in internal and external harmony with nature is meaningful. Religious fantasies about a soft life far away from your actual life here on Earth is not realistic.

I encourage young people like yourself to learn the Universal Way and become part of a new spiritual species in the world, a species that is not violent, does not do drugs, is not dependent upon alcohol and makes no trouble for itself or others, and is open to continual spiritual learning.

Trans-religion is the fundamental perspective that I recommend to all people. Although you were born into a certain society with its own customs, it is important to be open and receptive to other ways of life. The great variety of cultural and religious teachings in the world all express the important and abundant achievements of human life.

Religious teachings were services to the masses in the past, but they do not offer substantial support to your personal spiritual development. no individual who truly achieved themselves, such as Mahavira Jina (the founder of Jainism), Sakyamuni, Jesus, Abraham, Moses and Mohammed, belonged to any religion after attaining their own experience; however, the spiritual truths that they emphasized were turned into popular religions that served the masses. The religion is not the truth; the spiritual development and real experience of these achieved ones is the truth. Anyone who achieves themselves will be no less than the religious heroes or spiritual leaders of the past.

It can be helpful to regard all religions as equal and consider them as customs. The path of spiritual self-cultivation is different than an external religion. It serves those who are already developed enough to be able to serve themselves rather than continue a habitual reliance on a teacher or government or church. outgrowing one's own self-obstructions depends on individual effort, spiritual self-cultivation and personal growth.

I offer my spiritual friendship and support to all individuals who are willing to work on the important aspects of their lives. I serve the masses also, but only by promoting the spiritual development of all individuals. I do not brand cows so that everyone will know whose ranch the herd belongs to. I do not do anything that would divide society. I prefer to guide people to build a harmonious, universal society in which great individuals help the world become a better place in which to live.

Shambhala Sun: Thank you very much.

VIII
General Religion vs. the Universal Way

The following supplement is meant to help the public understand the difference between general religions and the Universal Way of Natural Spiritual Development. It also distinguishes between general culture and the Universal Way. I recommend that all individuals practice spiritual self-cultivation and break down the barriers between world religions, like so many Berlin Walls. Religions are social customs that offer neither spiritual growth to individuals nor social progress to the world.

1. *Religions worship God or an "initiator."*

The Universal Way of Natural Spiritual Development is not an external form of worship, it is an internal process of discovery that was developed by self-realization. The ancient spiritually developed ones truly knew that all natural life has a spiritual sphere. Only when you truly develop yourself spiritually do you know that individual life has the same natural spiritual reality as universal life. Your internal spiritual experience and the external world are not two separate realms.

2. *Religions misrepresent the natural spiritual reality as a hierarchical form of government with a supreme ruler who is able to be pleased or bribed in return for special favors. A human soul can receive grace or special privileges based on how well it attracts God's attention.*

The Universal Way of Natural Spiritual Development respects the spiritual reality in oneself, which is the innate reality of all natural life. There is no external authority that needs to be pleased. You have already received the grace of life by being born with all three spheres of body, mind and spirit. A peaceful life that is aligned with universal subtle law is the way to everlasting life. If you ignore the universal subtle law by your own negative behavior, the resulting disadvantage is self-created. Spiritual richness, nobility and creativity is your spiritual potential for bringing goodness into the world. One whose life is self-united is a real divine being who lives in the world.

3. *Religions worship their own founders as universal rulers or as divinities or as divine messengers of God.*

The Universal Way of Natural Spiritual Development recognizes that, at different times and different places, any talented people who make a humanistic contribution are divine. Divinity is not limited to spiritual teachers, prophets or saints. The most valuable spiritual contribution of any time is to bring peace to the world. Other practical improvements such as great inventions are also valuable. We respect all humanistic contributions and recognize the gifted individuals who make them, regardless of their age, race, gender or religion. Nor do we limit our worship to people who have died. In other words, religions worship a divinity that they have set up for you, while the Universal Way of Natural Spiritual

Development respects whoever you can learn from as a living spiritual activity.

4. *Religions usually base their beliefs and codes of behavior on a particular book of scripture and regard the contents of that book as the supreme truth.*

The Universal Way of Natural Spiritual Development is based upon the plain truth and encourages open investigation. It is there to help you freely explore both external and internal nature in order to further your own growth. The natural truth is beyond any ideology, which at best is only a good description. Your direct experience and achievement are what determine your true identity. An external religion is not your identity.

5. *Religions usually depend upon a priesthood, church, temple, ashram, mosque, etc. for material support, and thus require their followers to commit themselves to playing a role either as an officiant or a member of the congregation.*

The Universal Way of Natural Spiritual Development promotes a decent life that includes appropriate life activities, not rigid rules or prohibitions. You are not committed to a formula, you are committed to a natural healthy life with good spirits inside of you. Once such subtle attainment is achieved, a person becomes naturally harmonious, positive, creative, helpful and serviceable.

Priesthoods, churches, ashrams, etc. are the playground of an undeveloped mind. If you take them too seriously, you never develop beyond idol worship, because you never attain real personal growth.

6. *Religions make you financially responsible for supporting their activities by making substantial donations to them on a regular basis.*

Teachers and workers of the Universal Way of Natural Spiritual Development must be self-supporting and offer their services voluntarily. There is no spiritual or financial obligation between teachers and learners. Teachers and workers can certainly charge fairly for their work; all good work must be supported so that good workers are not abused. People of sincere and deep understanding are encouraged to become involved in teaching, but we do not ask for donations in order to accomplish our spiritual tasks.

7. *Religions have a figurehead such as a pope or a patriarch, an ayatollah or a caliph, a karmapa or a dalai lama, etc.*

The Universal Way of Natural Spiritual Development places no one in a position of self-aggrandizement, because doing so would degrade the natural spiritual quality of the individual. The Eastern term "master" does not imply a high social status. The American use of the word master signified an educator or instructor. In the Universal Way, the term master connotes mastery over oneself. If people insist upon calling a teacher master, this does not establish any kind of master-slave relationship between the teacher and the student, which is a spiritual friendship. Each enjoys his or her natural development as a human being. This is the reason all people should come together as friends.

8. *Religions originate from the human mind. Ancient religions continue to live on because of the support they receive from custom and convention.*

The Universal Way of Natural Spiritual Development distinguishes clearly between what is artificial and what is natural. Nothing that is man made is good at all times and in all places. The Universal Way is based on the universal flow of all lives, thus we are not confused by passing fashions. We know what can and cannot be changed. An example of what cannot be changed is the natural functions of the body; can a person use their nostrils for eating or their ears for breathing? Human development always faces change, both good and bad, but the basic foundation of being human does not change.

We respect the natural inspiration that is revealed in the *I Ching*, the *Tao Teh Ching*, etc. They do not teach people to be egotistic or lean upon any religion; they teach them the principles of natural life. This is different from working toward amassing social influence or power.

9. *Religions are based on mythological stories that are taken as fact. Occasionally the mythology holds up as a metaphor, but it still does not present the truth directly.*

The Universal Way of Natural Spiritual Development teaches the direct truth that comes from the spiritual development and discoveries of special individuals of different generations. When you follow the same processes that they have followed, you will make the same discoveries.

10. *Religions have only one level: the undeveloped mind. They play and manipulate the mind. They create a psychological substitute to replace the essence of life. It is not truthful development.*

The teaching of the Universal Way of Natural Spiritual Development contains three levels of responsibility for all individuals: the healthy development of body, mind and spirit. These are valuable arts that can help one develop all three spheres and achieve a complete life.

Religions do not value the art of physical exercise, they ignore people's physical health. To overlook the natural physical reality of life and universal nature while they talk about the universal ruler is a trick of the imagination. The Universe has no ruler, but the universal subtle law rules even divine lives.

11. *Religions consider spiritual life and secular life to be two separate things. They devalue secular life and respect only the spiritual life.*

Spiritual development assists the individual's secular life. Secular life takes its value from spiritual life. There is no real separation between what is called world and what is called spiritual. Such a division is based on an incomplete vision of life and nature.

12. *Religions serve the surface, social level of life. That level does not contain deep truth, but that is where they focus. Their main contribution is made at the emotional level.*

The Universal Way of Natural Spiritual Development is profound, it is not a system of belief or psychological manipulation. There must be true achievement. As a student of the Universal Way, you achieve true development step by step. Otherwise, without personal attainment, you would only be an appendage of an external social structure.

13. *Religions lack an objective foundation of spiritual truth. They even fear an objective approach.*

The University Way of Natural Spiritual Development welcomes objectivity. This was the means used by the ancient developed individuals when making their valuable attainments.

The Universal Way is deeply interested in guiding physically-oriented modern scholars and scientists to make a breakthrough in the meeting between the physical sciences and the universal spiritual reality of life. Although modern science is still fragmentary, it can still accomplish exploratory work toward an understanding of the ancient spiritual discoveries of life.

14. *Religions cannot really help people who are struggling with physical problems. They don't know that in some cases, physical problems originate from emotional or from spiritual problems.*

The Universal Way of Natural Spiritual Development includes natural healing, which allows miracles to happen by themselves. Such healing does not come from the power of any divine beings. The power for self-healing is a natural endowment of all life. All levels of individual personal health extend to the health of society, which is the focus of the Universal Way.

15. *Church and temple religions, etc., are narrow. They can only teach what their books say. The purpose of doing so is to bring in support to them.*

The Universal Way promotes broad universal spiritual learning to break down the borders of religions. It assists all people's spiritual growth. The Universal Way is a school from which you can graduate.

16. *Religions may call themselves spiritual schools, but you cannot graduate from them, and students can never rise higher than the teacher.*

The Universal Way of Natural Spiritual Development encourages the student to be better and do better than any previous or present models. Because it serves the spiritual development of all people, the Universal Way does not try to control people.

17. *Taoism, as it exists in China and abroad with Taoist masters and priests, presents itself as a religion.*

The Universal Way of Natural Spiritual Development treats Taoism as one of the world's religions, with all the limitations of a religion that depends on custom, convention and financial support from its followers. It is not my interest or intent to reform it. Yet, in all religion, there are some individuals who achieve independent understanding and personal attainment. They should leave the old shell behind and work to improve the world.

18. The Universal Way does not purposely present any tradition. It represents the individual effort of gathering the essence of beneficial human culture as the nutrition of life. The Universal Way re-evaluates all religions and all cultures in order to provide a better spiritual life for all people.

19. Very few individuals were true leaders of their time. Some of them bestowed a historical legacy to humanity, with everlasting spiritual value for generations to come.

The Universal Way respects any individual who teaches from a humanistic vision rather than from personal or social ambition. In the deepest sense, there are no truthful religions, but there are truthful individuals who teach. The Universal Way accepts them universally. The social structures that have adhered to their teachings can be overlooked.

20. The Universal Way takes spiritual support from millions of yers of human life experience. It does not encourage people to take pride in being a great teacher or heroic individual. The Universal Way encourages people to take pride in being a small teacher of great truth with everlasting value.

The Universal Way's persistent goal has been to provide a spiritual school that educates people in total health and well-being of the body, mind and spirit. This will enable the individual as well as society to bring spiritual benefit to the world and all people.

21. The Universal Way is the foundation of the Universal Society of the Integral Way. It is not bureaucratic, but it is a path of universal life in which people learn and work together in a spirit of harmony and service to spiritually heal all internal and external struggles.

This is the clear direction we set for ourselves and our teaching. This is the direction offered to all friends who wish to unite their own spirits with the universal spiritual reality, not in the sense of God, but in the sense of universal spiritual harmony.

22. If this seems like a lot to remember, you can simply remember that *Ni* means "people," *Hua* means "change to," and *Ching* means "spiritual purity, mental clarity and physical health." That is the simple goal of the teaching of the Universal Way.

Selected books by Hua-Ching Ni:

Selected Other Materials Available
from SevenStar Communications
on Natural Healing Arts and Sciences include:

Books
The Tao of Nutrition by Dr. Maoshing Ni
Chinese Vegetarian Delights by Lily Chuang
Chinese Herbology Made Easy by Dr. Maoshing Ni
Crane Style Chi Gong by Dr. Daoshing Ni
101 Vegetarian Delights by Lily Chuang and Cathy McNease

Pocket Booklets
Guide to Your Total Well-Being By Hua-Ching Ni
Progress Along the Way By Hua-Ching Ni
The Light of All Stars by Hua-Ching Ni
Less Stress, More Happiness
Integral Nutrition

Videotapes (VHS)
Attune Your Body with Dao-In by Hua-Ching Ni
T'ai Chi Chuan: An Appreciation by Hua-Ching Ni
Crane Style Chi Gong by Dr. Daoshing Ni
Self-Healing Chi Gong by Dr. Maoshing Ni
Eight Treasures by Dr. Maoshing Ni
T'ai Chi Chuan I & II by Dr. Maoshing Ni

Audiotapes (by Dr. Maoshing Ni)
Invocations: Health, Longevity & Healing a Broken Heart
Chi Gong for Stress Release
Chi Gong for Pain Management

SEVEN STAR
COMMUNICATIONS

If you wish to receive a copy of the latest SevenStar Communications catalog of books, booklets, videos and cassettes on alternative health topics, spiritual realization and movement arts, and to be placed on our mailing list, please call us at 310-576-1901 or fill out this page and mail it to:

SevenStar Communications
1314 Second Street
Santa Monica, CA 90401

(Please Print)

Name————————————————————————

Address ———————————————————————

City, State, Zip———————————————————

Country ————————————————————————

Spiritual Study and Teaching Through the College of Tao

The College of Tao (COT) and the Union of Tao and Man were formally established in California in the 1970's, yet this tradition is a very broad spiritual culture containing centuries of human spiritual growth. Its central goal is to offer healthy spiritual education to all people. The goal of the school is to help individuals develop themselves for a spiritually developed world. This time-tested school values the spiritual development of each individual self and passes down its guidance and experience.

COT is a school which has no walls. The big human society is its classroom. Your own life and service is the class you attend; thus students grow from their lives and from studying the guidance of the Universal Way.

Any interested individual is welcome to join and learn to grow for oneself. The Self-Study Program can be useful to you. The Program, which is based on Master Ni's books and videotapes, gives people who wish to study on their own or are too far from a volunteer teacher an opportunity to study the Way at their own speed. The outline for the Self-Study Program is in the book *The Golden Message*. If you choose, the Correspondence Course is also available.

A Mentor is any individual who is spiritually self-responsible and who sets up a model of a healthy and complete life for oneself and others. They may serve as teachers for general society and people with preliminary interest in spiritual development. To receive recognition from the USIW for teaching activity, a Mentor must first register with the USIW and follow the Mentor Service Handbook which was written by Mentors. They can teach special skills which are certified by the USIW. It is recommended that all students use the Correspondence Course or self-study program to educate themselves to be Mentors, but students also may learn directly from a Mentors. COT also offers special seminars which are taught only to Mentors.

- -

If you are interested in the Integral Way Correspondence Course/Self-Study Program, please write: College of Tao, PO Box 1222, El Prado, NM 87529.

- -

Mail to: USIW, PO Box 28993, Atlanta, GA 30358-0993

_____ I wish to be put on the mailing list of the USIW to be notified of educational activities.

_____ I wish to receive a list of Registered Mentors teaching in my area or country.

_____ I am interested in joining /forming a study group in my area.

_____ I am interested in becoming a Mentor of the USIW.

Name:_____

Address:_____

City:_____ State:_____ Zip:_____